SENDCB

First published in 2024

Copyright

This book is sold subject to the condition that it shall not, by way of trade or otherwise, be lent, resold, hired out or otherwise circulated in any form of binding or cover other than that in which it is published without the publisher's prior consent.

Photocopy licence

The material in this book is protected by copyright. However, the purchaser is free to make copies of particular articles for instructions.

Disclaimer

This book was written in my voice and is based on the experiences I had while working in the field of education.

SENDCB

SENDCB

To my amazing nephew, Kareem who is often misunderstood, this book is for you. I hope you get all the help and support that you need to make your school life fun and manageable.

Love you millions
Aunty Cand xx

Contents

1. Introduction
3. Understanding Special Educational Needs
6. Negative beliefs and stigmas
7. SEND code of practice
9. Areas of need
11. The SEN register and SEN support
12. The graduated approach
14. Roles and responsibilities
20. Education, Health and Care Plans
23. What goes into an EHCP?
24. Types of schools
26. EOTAS: Education other than at school
28. Mediations and tribunals: The process
29. Making an appeal
30. Changing attitudes in society
31. Autism Spectrum Disorder (ASD)
33. How does Autism affect learning?
34. Pathological Demand Avoidance (PDA)
36. Attention Deficit Hyperactivity Disorder (ADHD)
38. Digging deeper into ADHD
39. School based anxiety
43. Developmental Co-ordination Disorder (Dyspraxia)
44. How does DCD affect learning?
46. Dyscalculia
47. Dyslexia
48. Speech & Language disorders
50. Sensory Processing Disorder (SPD)
51. Visual Impairment
52. Attachment Disorder
53. Acronyms
54. Bibliography and references
55. Thank you

INTRODUCTION
sendcb.co.uk

Special educational needs refers to diverse learning requirements that require additional support and accommodations for students to thrive academically and socially.

In the UK, the proportion of students with special educational needs (SEN) rose to 1.57 million students in 2023, or 17.3% of all students. The number of students with SEN had been declining since 2010 (21.1%), but it has been rising over the past six years.

According to the UK Government's official statistics, the most common special educational needs in the UK are specific Learning Difficulties (such as Dyslexia), Speech, Language, and Communication needs, and Autism Spectrum Disorder.

The Essential Guide to Special Educational Needs is the must-have book for:
- Parents and carers
- Teachers, teaching assistants, and school leaders
- Healthcare professionals
- Doctors and nurses
- Employers
- Students
- Anyone interested in learning about special educational needs

This book explains complex topics in simple terms, making it easy for both beginners and experts to understand.

I hope this book makes your days (and nights) a little easier.
Candace x

UNDERSTANDING
SPECIAL EDUCATIONAL NEEDS

SEND stands for Special Educational Needs and Disabilities. It refers to a wide range of challenges or conditions that children and young people may have which affect their ability to learn or participate in school in the same way as their peers. These challenges can include physical disabilities, learning difficulties, sensory impairments (such as sight or hearing problems), communication disorders, and developmental conditions like autism spectrum disorder.

When a child has SEND, it means they may need extra support, resources, or adjustments in their education to help them succeed. This could involve personalised teaching methods, additional learning materials, assistive technology, or accommodations to make the school environment more accessible.

Somebody with a 'special need' may have physical, emotional or behavioural difficulties that make it harder for them to learn, compared to others of the same age.

SEND affects children and young people of all ages, backgrounds, and abilities. It can be present from birth or develop later in life due to genetic factors, medical conditions, environmental influences, or accidents. SEND is not limited to a specific demographic group and can impact individuals from all socioeconomic backgrounds and cultural identities.

Recognising and addressing SEND is essential to ensure that affected children and young people receive the appropriate support and accommodations to reach their full potential in education and beyond. This typically involves collaboration between parents, schools, healthcare professionals, and specialists to develop personalised strategies and interventions tailored to each child's unique needs.

UNDERSTANDING SPECIAL EDUCATIONAL NEEDS

Estimating the precise number of people worldwide with special needs presents challenges due to several factors:

1. Diverse Range of Special Needs: Special needs encompass a broad spectrum of conditions, including physical disabilities, intellectual impairments, sensory limitations, learning difficulties, and mental health disorders, among others.

2. Varied Definitions: Definitions of "special needs" may differ across countries, regions, and organisations, complicating efforts to provide an exact count.

3. Underreporting and Data Gaps: In numerous parts of the world, disabilities might be underreported due to stigma, limited access to healthcare, or insufficient data collection methods.

However, according to the World Health Organisation (WHO), over one billion people, or roughly 15% of the global population, live with some form of disability. This figure encompasses a wide array of conditions and does not exclusively focus on what might conventionally be termed "special needs."

In essence, while there's no precise tally for the global population with special needs, it's evident that a substantial portion of humanity is affected by various disabilities or special requirements.

LET'S DIG A LITTLE DEEPER

The way we support people with special needs in education has come a long way, reflecting how people's attitudes toward disabilities have changed over time.

Let's take a quick look at the key moments leading up to 2024:

1. **Early History:** Historically, individuals with disabilities faced marginalisation and limited access to education and support services.

2. **19th Century:** Early interventions by pioneers like Jean-Marc-Gaspard Itard and Maria Montessori emphasised personalised approaches to education for individuals with disabilities.

3. **20th Century:** The 20th century witnessed the rise and fall of the eugenics movement, alongside increasing advocacy efforts for disability rights and access to education.

4. **1940s-1950s:** This era saw the establishment of specialised schools and programs for individuals with disabilities in many countries.

5. **1960s-1970s:** The civil rights and disability rights movements gained momentum, leading to legislative changes like the Education for All Handicapped Children Act (EAHCA) of 1975 in the United States.

6. **1980s-1990s:** The Individuals with Disabilities Education Act (IDEA) of 1990 further strengthened the rights of individuals with disabilities and mandated individualised education plans (IEPs).

7. **21st Century:** Inclusive education practices became more prevalent, focusing on mainstreaming and inclusion of students with disabilities in general education classrooms. Advances in technology also improved accessibility through assistive technologies.

8. **Global Perspectives:** Internationally, there was a growing recognition of the rights of individuals with disabilities, leading to the adoption of international agreements like the United Nations Convention on the Rights of Persons with Disabilities (CRPD).

9. **2024 and Beyond:** The landscape of special needs education continues to evolve, with ongoing efforts to promote inclusive education, address systemic barriers, and ensure equitable access to education for all individuals, regardless of ability. Advocates strive for greater awareness, support, and opportunities for individuals with disabilities in education and beyond.

NEGATIVE BELIEFS AND
STIGMAS

It has been reported that students with special needs have encountered various negative attitudes and beliefs, known as stigmas. These stigmas include:

1. **Assuming They Can't Do Things:** Some people think that students with special needs can't do things as well as others without disabilities.

2. **Feeling Left Out:** Students with special needs may feel left out or not included in social activities because they're different from their peers.

3. **Being Bullied:** They might get picked on or bullied by others because of their differences, which can make them feel bad about themselves.

4. **Pity or Feeling Sorry:** Some people treat students with special needs like they should be pitied or feel sorry for them, instead of seeing them as capable individuals.

5. **Not Being Given Chances:** There's a belief that students with special needs don't have the same chances to succeed as others, so they might not get the same opportunities to learn and grow.

6. **Being Labelled:** When someone is labelled with a specific disability, people might assume things about them instead of seeing their unique strengths and talents.

"What negative attitudes mean to me is that it makes me feel really angry that people discriminate towards people with a learning disability because they think I don't have a meaningful life like everybody else has."
Harry Roche

7. **Depending on Others:** People might think that students with special needs always need help from others and can't do things on their own.

8. **Being Kept Apart:** Sometimes, students with special needs are kept separate from other students, which makes them feel different and left out.

9. **Not Being Understood:** People might not understand what it's like to have a disability, so they treat students with special needs differently or unfairly.

10. **Not Believing in Their Potential:** Some people don't think that students with special needs can achieve as much as others, so they don't give them the same chances to succeed.

These negative attitudes and beliefs can hurt the feelings and confidence of students with special needs, making it harder for them to feel included and accepted in school and society.

SEND CODE OF PRACTICE

The SEND Code of Practice is a statutory guidance document in the United Kingdom that provides advice to local authorities, schools, and other institutions on supporting children and young people with special educational needs and disabilities from birth to the age of 25.

Legal Guidance:
The SEND Code of Practice is a statutory document in the UK, meaning it has legal force and provides guidance that must be followed by schools, local authorities, and other relevant agencies when supporting children and young people with SEND.

Age Range:
The Code covers individuals from birth to the age of 25, recognising that support for SEND should be provided across different stages of development, from early years through to adulthood.

Inclusive Approach:
It emphasises the importance of inclusive education and promoting practices that enable all students, regardless of their SEND status, to fully participate in education and achieve their potential.

Collaboration:
The Code emphasises the need for collaboration between education, health, and social care professionals, as well as involving parents and carers in decision-making processes, to ensure that support for individuals with SEND is coordinated and effective.

Terminology:
In the SEND Code of Practice, "must" indicates legal obligations that must be followed, while "should" denotes strong recommendations or best practices. Compliance with "must" statements is mandatory and failure to do so may lead to legal consequences. "Should" statements, although not legally binding, are considered important and are expected to be followed unless there's a valid reason not to.

The SEND Code of Practice guides various stakeholders in supporting children and young people with special educational needs and disabilities.

SEND CODE OF PRACTICE

Special educational needs and disability code of practice: 0 to 25 years

Statutory guidance for organisations who work with and support children and young people with special educational needs and disabilities

July 2014

~~~~~~~

This includes schools, local authorities, health and social care professionals, parents, and education professionals.
Schools use the Code to identify, assess, and support students with SEND, ensuring appropriate interventions for academic and social success. Local authorities refer to the Code to fulfil legal obligations in providing support services, coordinating services and funding.

Health and social care professionals use it to understand their roles and collaborate for holistic care. Parents and carers rely on the Code to understand their rights, access support, and advocate for their children.

Education professionals, like teachers and SENCOs, use it to meet diverse student needs effectively. Overall, the Code provides crucial guidance on best practices, legal requirements, and collaborative approaches for inclusive education and holistic support for individuals with SEND.

AREAS OF NEED

In the context of Special Educational Needs and Disabilities, there are four broad areas of need that encompass different types of challenges or difficulties that children and young people may experience. These areas are defined in the SEND Code of Practice, which provides guidance for identifying and supporting individuals with SEND. Here are the four areas of need and how they can affect learning:

1. Communication and Interaction:

This area includes difficulties with speech, language, and communication skills, as well as challenges with social interaction and understanding social cues.

Impact on Learning:
Children with communication and interaction needs may struggle to express themselves verbally, understand instructions, or engage in conversations. This can affect their ability to communicate effectively with teachers and peers, participate in classroom activities, and access the curriculum. Difficulties with social interaction may also lead to feelings of isolation and hinder collaboration with others.

2. Cognition and Learning:

This area encompasses a wide range of learning difficulties, including specific learning difficulties like dyslexia and dyscalculia, as well as general cognitive impairments that affect information processing and academic progress.

Impact on Learning: Children with cognition and learning needs may have difficulty acquiring and retaining new information, understanding abstract concepts, or applying knowledge to different contexts. They may struggle with tasks such as reading, writing, mathematics, and problem-solving. These difficulties can hinder their progress in school and require tailored teaching approaches, additional support, and accommodations to address their individual learning styles and needs.

AREAS OF NEED

3. Social, Emotional, and Mental Health (SEMH):
This area encompasses challenges related to emotional regulation, mental health conditions, and social and behavioural difficulties that affect a child's well-being and relationships with others.

Impact on Learning: Children with SEMH needs may experience anxiety, depression, low self-esteem, or behavioural issues that impact their ability to concentrate, engage in learning activities, and participate positively in the classroom environment. These challenges can lead to disruptions in learning, poor attendance, and difficulties forming friendships. Supporting children's social, emotional, and mental health is essential for creating a positive and inclusive learning environment where all students feel valued, supported, and able to thrive.

4. Sensory and/or Physical Needs:
This area includes difficulties related to sensory impairments (such as visual or hearing impairments) and physical disabilities that affect mobility, coordination, or access to learning materials and environments.

Impact on Learning: Children with sensory and/or physical needs may require adaptations, accommodations, or specialised equipment to access learning materials, participate in activities, and navigate the school environment. For example, students with visual impairments may need braille materials or screen readers, while those with physical disabilities may require wheelchair-accessible facilities and assistive devices. Ensuring a physically accessible and inclusive environment is essential for enabling these students to fully engage in learning activities and reach their educational goals.

Understanding and addressing the diverse needs within these four areas is essential for providing inclusive and effective support to children and young people with SEND. By recognising individual strengths and challenges, implementing tailored interventions, and fostering a supportive learning environment, educators and professionals can help all students achieve their full potential.

THE SEN REGISTER AND SEN SUPPORT

The Special Needs Register is a record kept by schools in the UK of students who have been identified as having special educational needs. Students with SEN are placed on this register to ensure that their specific needs and requirements are recognised and addressed within the school system.

Students may be placed on the Special Needs Register if they require additional support in their learning due to factors such as:

1. Learning difficulties, such as dyslexia or dyscalculia.
2. Communication or language disorders.
3. Autism spectrum disorder or other developmental disorders.
4. Social, emotional, or mental health needs.
5. Sensory impairments (e.g., hearing or vision impairments).
6. Physical disabilities or medical conditions that impact their ability to learn.

All schools and colleges operate differently, but the general placement of a child on the Special Needs Register is based on assessments conducted by teachers, educational psychologists, health professionals, or other specialists, which identify the student's specific needs and determine the level of support required. The register helps schools to effectively plan and deliver targeted support for students with SEN, ensuring that their individual needs are met and that they can fully participate in education alongside their peers.

SEN Support

The Code of Practice 2015 introduced a new category known as SEN Support, which replaced the previous School Action and School Action Plus. Alongside this change, a graduated approach called Assess, Plan, Do, Review was implemented to address learning barriers and provide effective provision.

SEN Support, short for Special Educational Needs support, refers to the services and resources offered to students with special educational needs. These needs may encompass learning disabilities, physical impairments, communication difficulties, sensory issues, or emotional and behavioural disorders.

THE GRADUATED APPROACH

The Graduated Approach, often referred to as **Assess, Plan, Do, Review (APDR)**, is a framework used in the UK to support children and young people with Special Educational Needs and Disabilities in schools. It's outlined in the Special Educational Needs and Disability Code of Practice (SEND Code of Practice) and is designed to ensure a systematic and structured approach to identifying and meeting the needs of children with SEND. Here's an overview of each stage:

Assess essentially means taking a close look at a student to understand what they're good at and where they might need extra help. Teachers do this by observing how the student learns, chatting with their teachers and parents to get more insights, and sometimes doing specific tests or activities to figure out their strengths and challenges. This assessment phase helps teachers get a clear picture of the student's needs so they can come up with the best plan to support them in their learning journey. Based on the assessment findings, a tailored support plan is developed to address the child's identified needs and support their progress in education.

The plan is developed collaboratively with input from teachers, SENCOs (Special Educational Needs Coordinators), parents, and any other professionals involved. It outlines the specific interventions, strategies, and accommodations that will be put in place to support the child's learning and development.

The support plan sets clear objectives, targets, and actions to be implemented to meet the child's needs. It may include provisions for additional resources, specialised teaching approaches, adaptations to the curriculum, or access to support services.

Plan involves creating a personalised strategy to address the specific needs identified during the assessment phase. This plan outlines the actions and interventions that will be put in place to support the student's learning and development. It may include setting specific goals, determining the resources and support needed, and outlining the roles and responsibilities of everyone involved, such as teachers, parents, and specialists.

Once the plan is established, the "do" phase involves implementing the planned interventions and support strategies in the classroom and other learning environments.

THE GRADUATED APPROACH
continued

Do in the graduated approach cycle involves putting the plans into action and implementing strategies and interventions to support learning and development. It requires closely monitoring progress and making necessary adjustments to ensure the individual's needs are effectively met.

Review involves looking back at how well the strategies and interventions put in place during the "do" stage worked. This includes checking the progress the person has made, listening to feedback from teachers, parents, and others involved, and deciding what needs to be changed or improved to better support their needs.

The effectiveness of the support plan and interventions is evaluated through regular reviews to ensure that the child's needs are being met and that progress is being made.

Reviews are typically conducted at least annually, although they may occur more frequently if needed. They involve gathering feedback from all stakeholders, reviewing progress against the objectives and targets set out in the support plan, and identifying any necessary adjustments or changes to the support provision.

The review process informs ongoing decision-making about the child's support needs. It may result in revisions to the support plan, changes to interventions or accommodations, or referrals for further assessment or specialist support if required.

Overall, the Graduated Approach, through its **Assess, Plan, Do, Review** cycle, provides a structured framework for identifying, planning, implementing, and reviewing support for children and young people with SEND in schools. It promotes collaboration, transparency, and accountability among all stakeholders involved in supporting the child's learning and development.

ROLES AND RESPONSIBILITES

Working with children and young people with special needs requires a different set of skills than working with those without disabilities. Each child with special needs is unique, but there are some general practices to keep in mind to make sure they feel comfortable and engaged.

There are various roles within the field of special needs, including:

Special Educational Needs Coordinator (SENDCO)
SENCOs, or Special Educational Needs Coordinators, are the heart of a school's support system for students with special educational needs. They are qualified teachers who work closely with teachers, parents, and external professionals to identify and address the individual needs of these students.

This involves developing clear policies and procedures to ensure consistent support and accommodations are provided throughout the school. SENCOs coordinate interventions and support strategies, tailor them to each student's needs, and regularly review their effectiveness.

They also provide guidance and support to teachers, ensuring they have the necessary skills to meet the diverse needs of their students

Additionally, SENCOs serve as a point of contact for parents, involving them in decision-making processes and keeping them informed of their child's progress.

SENCOs play a crucial role in fostering an inclusive learning environment where all students have the opportunity to thrive.

In the United Kingdom, individuals who are qualified teachers or have relevant experience in education can become Special Educational Needs Coordinators. Typically, the following requirements apply:

Qualified Teacher Status (QTS): Most schools require SENCOs to hold QTS, which is obtained through completing an accredited teacher training programme.

National Award for Special Educational Needs Coordination (NASENCO):
The National Award for Special Educational Needs Coordination is a mandatory postgraduate qualification for SENCOs in mainstream schools in the UK, designed to enhance their knowledge and skills in managing and supporting pupils with special educational needs.

ROLES AND RESPONSIBILITES

Additional Training: Some schools may offer or require additional training in special educational needs coordination.

Experience: While not always a strict requirement, schools often prefer SENCOs with prior teaching experience, particularly in special educational needs or inclusive education settings.

Knowledge: SENCOs should have a good understanding of special educational needs legislation, policies, and best practices for supporting students with SEN.

Skills: Strong communication, organisation, and interpersonal skills are essential for SENCOs, as they work closely with teachers, parents, and external agencies to coordinate support for students with SEN.

Overall, while specific requirements may vary depending on the school or local authority, individuals interested in becoming SENCOs should possess a combination of teaching qualifications, relevant experience, and a commitment to supporting students with special educational needs effectively.

ROLES AND RESPONSIBILITES

Special Education Teacher (SEN Teacher)

A special needs teacher is someone who dedicates themselves to supporting students with various challenges in their learning journey. They work closely with students who may have different abilities, ensuring that each individual receives the attention and assistance they need to thrive academically and emotionally. These teachers go above and beyond to create inclusive and supportive learning environments, where every student feels valued and empowered to reach their full potential. They collaborate with other educators, parents, and specialists to tailor teaching strategies and provide personalised support, ensuring that every student's unique needs are met. Through their compassion, dedication, and expertise, special needs teachers make a profound difference in the lives of their students, helping them overcome obstacles and achieve success in school and beyond.

Teaching Assistant (TA)

A Teaching Assistant provides support to the classroom teacher and students who have learning disabilities and/or additional needs. TAs can work in special schools (supporting children with severe or complex special educational needs) or with individual pupils or small groups in mainstream classes.

They assist with preparing resources, breaking down information for better understanding, facilitating interventions, updating paperwork, and providing feedback to other staff members..

In the United Kingdom, Teaching Assistants play a vital role in inclusive education, ensuring that all students, including those with special educational needs and disabilities, receive appropriate support to access the curriculum and participate fully in school life.

TA's collaborate closely with teachers, SENCOs, and other professionals to implement individual education plans (IEPs) and provide tailored support to students with SEND. They may also assist in creating a supportive and inclusive learning environment, adapting teaching materials, and providing one-to-one or small group support to students who require additional assistance. Overall, TAs contribute significantly to the academic and social development of students with SEND, helping them to achieve their full potential.

ROLES AND RESPONSIBILITES

Speech and Language Therapist (SALT)

A Speech and Language Therapist, also known as a Speech and Language Pathologist, is a professional who specialises in assessing and treating communication disorders, including speech, language, and swallowing difficulties. In the context of special educational needs and disabilities, SALTs play a crucial role in supporting individuals with communication impairments.

For individuals with SEND, communication difficulties can significantly impact their ability to participate in educational and social activities, as well as their overall quality of life. SALTs work with these individuals to assess their communication needs, develop personalised intervention plans, and provide therapy to improve their communication skills.

ROLES AND RESPONSIBILITES

Educational Psychologist (EP)

Educational Psychologists are specialists who focus on understanding how children and adolescents learn and grow in educational environments. They utilise their knowledge of psychology to enhance the educational, emotional, and social welfare of individuals with special needs.

Found predominantly in educational settings like schools and colleges, Educational Psychologists collaborate with various professionals involved in supporting individuals with special needs.

Their responsibilities encompass conducting assessments, implementing interventions, offering guidance on educational plans and curriculum adjustments, and fostering partnerships with teachers, parents, and other stakeholders. Ultimately, their aim is to facilitate the holistic development and inclusivity of individuals with special needs.

Occupational Therapist (OT)

The role of an Occupational Therapist in SEND is to help children and young people develop the skills they need to participate in daily activities, achieve their educational goals, and lead fulfilling lives to the best of their abilities.

Occupational Therapists assess individuals' strengths and challenges in areas like fine motor skills, handwriting, sensory processing, and daily living tasks. They collaboratively set goals to enhance independence and participation in school activities.

They design targeted interventions, collaborate with teachers and parents to integrate strategies into the educational plan, and provide training on effective support methods. They may recommend assistive technology and facilitate transitions between school levels while monitoring progress and adjusting interventions as needed.

ROLES AND RESPONSIBILITES

EHCP coordinator

Various names for this role exist across the country.

An EHC Coordinator is a specialist who assists in the development and administration of EHCPs for young people with special educational needs or disabilities. They collaborate with a range of stakeholders, including parents and carers, educators, health care providers, and social workers, while working in local authorities or educational environments. EHCP Coordinators take charge of gathering information, coordinating assessments, and drafting EHCPs to understand a child's needs thoroughly. They ensure the plans are properly put into action to support the child's education and development. They also assess the child's progress and make any necessary changes to the plans following annual reviews.

For educators and support staff, working in the field of SEND can be demanding and very stressful. The wide range of needs and abilities among students, which requires individualised attention and support, is one primary cause of stress. Because of this variety, it may be difficult to successfully address each student's demands. Teachers may also become frustrated due to lack resources and financial support for SEND resources.

Their capacity to give their pupils the finest education possible may be affected by their inability to get the necessary support, equipment, or professional help.

Stress can also be increased by navigating the complex legal and administrative procedures associated with SEND provision, included in EHCPs, assessments, and parent and agency meetings. For educators, the paperwork and administration involved with these procedures can be tedious and stressful. Despite these difficulties, working in SEND can be very rewarding because it gives educators the chance to significantly impact the lives of their pupils. However, in order to support staff in efficiently managing the challenges involved with working in SEND, sufficient support, training and resources must be provided.

EDUCATION, HEALTH AND CARE PLANS

A child may need an Education, Health and Care Plan if they have significant or complex special educational needs that cannot be adequately met by the support available in mainstream education settings. This may include children with disabilities, learning difficulties, or social, emotional, and mental health needs that require additional support and specialised provision. The decision to issue an EHCP is made through a formal assessment process carried out by the local authority involving professionals, parents/carers, and the child.

As of 20th July 2023, the number of children and young people with EHCP's increased to 389,171 in schools in England. Up by 9.5% from 2022.

A child needs to be academically 'behind' in order to have an EHCP is a common myth told to families by professionals.

An **EHCP** stands for Education, Health and Care Plan. It is a legal document in the United Kingdom that outlines the special educational needs and the support required by a child or young person up to the age of 25. It is used to ensure that the individual's education, health, and social care needs are understood and properly met.

Anyone can apply for an EHCP if they believe a child or young person requires additional support beyond what is typically available in school. This includes:

Parents and Carers: Often, parents are the primary advocates for their child's educational needs and may initiate the EHCP process if they feel their child requires extra support.

Schools and Educational Professionals: Teachers, SENCOs, and other educational professionals may request an EHCP assessment if they believe a student's needs cannot be adequately met through the school's resources and support systems.

The beauty of an EHCP is that it looks at a child/young person's needs holistically, covering Education, Health and Care. It is not specifically targeting a child's intellectual ability.

Healthcare Professionals: Doctors, therapists, and other healthcare providers may also recommend an EHCP assessment if they identify significant health-related needs impacting a child's education.

Local Authorities: In some cases, local authorities may initiate an EHCP assessment based on concerns raised by professionals or observations of a child's needs.

EDUCATION, HEALTH AND CARE PLANS

THE TIMELINE ↘

THE EHCP PROCESS TYPICALLY SPANS 20 WEEKS AND INVOLVES SEVERAL KEY STAGES:

Decision to Assess (Weeks 1-6):
- A parent or school requests an EHC Needs Assessment, initiating the EHCP process.
- Within six weeks, the local authority (LA) decides whether to proceed with the assessment. If denied, an appeal to SENDIST can be made within two months.

Assessment & Evidence Gathering (Weeks 6-12):
- The LA contacts relevant parties for information, including parents, schools, and healthcare professionals.
- By week 12, the LA decides whether to issue an EHCP based on the gathered evidence.

Drafting the EHC Plan (Weeks 13-16):
- If approved, the LA drafts the EHCP and sends a copy to parents and contributors for review.
- Parents have 15 days to provide feedback and request changes.

Issuing the EHC Plan (Weeks 17-20):
- Between weeks 17 and 20, the final EHCP is issued, including details of the child's support and school placement.
- Parents receive a letter outlining their right to appeal any EHCP decisions they disagree with.

It's important to note that the 20-week deadline is a legal requirement, and any extensions beyond this must be justified by specific exceptions. Delays due to waiting lists or staff shortages are not lawful reasons for extending the process.

The aim is to make decisions as promptly as possible within the 20-week timeframe.

EDUCATION, HEALTH AND CARE PLANS

THE TIMELINE

TWO COMMON MYTHS ABOUT EHCPS ARE:

1. EHCPs Guarantee Access to Specialist Provision: While EHCPs outline the support a child or young person needs, they do not automatically guarantee access to specialist provision or resources.
The provision outlined in an EHCP is based on an assessment of the child's needs and available resources within the local authority. In some cases, obtaining the desired provision may require additional advocacy or appeal processes.

2. EHCPs Are Only for Children with Severe Disabilities: There is a misconception that EHCPs are only for children with severe disabilities or complex needs. However, EHCPs are intended to support children and young people with a wide range of needs, including learning difficulties, medical conditions, sensory impairments, and social or emotional challenges. The key criteria for obtaining an EHCP is whether the child requires additional support beyond what is typically available in school to access education and achieve their full potential.

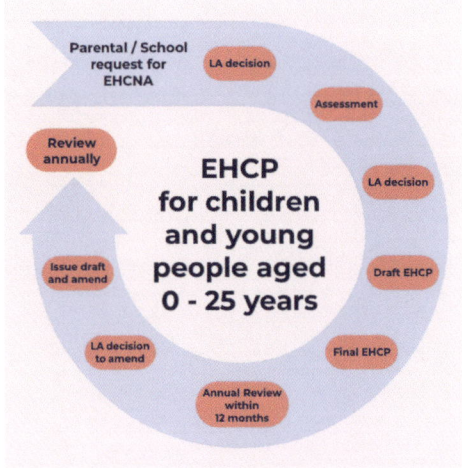

Image taken from: sossen.org.uk

WHAT GOES INTO AN EHCP?

> Education, health and care plans were introduced in England through the Children and Families Act 2014. The act came into effect in September 2014, making EHCPs a legal requirement for children and young people with special educational needs and disabilities (SEND) aged 0-25. EHCPs are designed to set out how education, health and social care services will work to meet the needs of the child or young person.
>
> They are produced by local authorities and have replaced statements of special educational needs. EHCPs should include the views of parents and the children or young people.

Here's a summary of what goes into an EHCP:

Section A contains the views, interests and aspirations of the child and his parents or the young person.

Section B gives a detailed look at the special educational needs of a child or young person.
- Description of the young person's SEN
- Assessment Information
- Areas of Strengths and SEN Needs

Section C describes educational needs, input from educational and healthcare specialists.

Section D contains any social care needs which relate to their SEN or to a disability.

Section E lists the planned outcomes or outcomes sought for the child or young person.

Section F relates to the special educational provision required to meet their SEN.

Section G includes any health care provision reasonably required by the learning difficulties or disabilities which result in the child or young person having SEN.

Section H contains any social care provision required from social services under the Chronically Sick and Disabled Persons Act 1970, and/or reasonably required by the learning difficulties or disabilities which result in the child or young person having SEN.

Section I will name of the school or other institution to be attended by the child or young person, and the type of that institution (or just the type if no specific institution is named).

Section J includes details of any direct payment which will be made.

Section K lists of all of the advice and information obtained as part of the EHC needs assessment or amended EHCP following an annual review.

TYPES OF **SCHOOLS**

Every child in England aged 5 to 16 has the right to attend a state school at no cost.
State schools obtain funding either from their local governing body or directly from the government. The following are the most prevalent types:

A mainstream school serves all students, regardless of their talents, disabilities, or special educational needs. It is sometimes referred to as an ordinary school or comprehensive school. To the greatest extent feasible, students with SEN attend mainstream schools with their peers without disabilities.

This is how SEN students are usually supported in mainstream schools:

Mainstream schools embrace inclusive education by integrating children with special educational needs into regular classrooms, fostering a sense of belonging and reducing segregation. They create individualised education plans or personal education plans for SEN students, tailored to their specific needs and goals, with collaboration between teachers, parents, and specialists. These schools appoint Special Educational Needs Coordinators (SENCOs) to oversee support provision and ensure appropriate interventions. Additional support such as teaching assistants, therapists, and counsellors is provided both inside and outside the classroom. Mainstream schools adapt curriculum, teaching methods, and materials to accommodate diverse needs, promoting accessibility through alternative formats and assistive technology. They prioritise social and emotional well-being, offering programs for peer interaction, social skills, and counselling, fostering confidence, resilience, and positive relationships among all students. Overall, mainstream schools are dedicated to providing a supportive, inclusive environment where all children, including those with SEN, can thrive academically, socially, and emotionally.

A resource base is a specialised facility within a mainstream school that offers extra support and resources for children with special educational needs. It is sometimes referred to as a resource provision or resource unit. Resource bases are made to meet the unique requirements of students who need extra help to access the curriculum and meet their learning objectives.

Resource bases within mainstream schools provide essential support for students with special educational needs. They employ specialised staff, such as teachers and teaching assistants, trained to assist SEN students with tailored instruction. Equipped with specific resources like adapted curriculum materials and assistive technology, these bases cater to the diverse learning needs of SEN students. Individualised education plans outline each student's goals and accommodations, with collaborative input from staff, parents, and professionals.

Despite their specialised focus, resource bases integrate SEN students into the broader school community, offering inclusive educational and social opportunities. Collaboration between resource bases and mainstream school staff ensures the full inclusion of SEN students in school activities, fostering their academic, social, and emotional development. Overall, resource bases are vital for supporting the educational inclusion of SEN students, facilitating their holistic growth and maximising their potential.

TYPES OF **SCHOOLS**

A special school is a dedicated educational institution specifically designed to cater to the needs of children and young people with special educational needs. These schools provide tailored support, resources, and facilities to meet the unique requirements of students with a wide range of disabilities, learning difficulties, and developmental disorders.

Here's how special schools typically support individuals with SEN:

Special schools cater specifically to students with special educational needs by offering a curriculum tailored to diverse learning styles and abilities. With small class sizes, students receive personalised attention from a multidisciplinary team of specialist staff, including therapists and psychologists. These schools provide therapeutic interventions, adaptive equipment, and facilities to support students' development and participation. Emphasising social and life skills, they prepare students for independence and inclusion in society through structured training and vocational education. Individualised education plans ensure targeted support, regularly reviewed in collaboration with parents and professionals. Overall, special schools create a nurturing environment where students with SEN can excel academically, socially, and emotionally, empowering them to achieve their full potential and lead fulfilling lives.

An independent school, also known as a private school or non-state school, is a school that is not funded or operated by the government. Instead, it is funded through tuition fees, donations, and endowments.

Independent schools have more autonomy over their curriculum, teaching methods, and policies compared to state-funded schools.

Here's how independent schools typically support students with special educational needs:

Independent schools provide tailored support to students with special educational needs, offering customised learning plans, specialised instruction, and additional resources to accommodate diverse learning styles. With smaller class sizes compared to state-funded schools, teachers can offer more individualised attention and targeted instruction, particularly beneficial for students with SEN. These schools often employ specialist staff, including special education teachers, therapists, and psychologists, who collaborate to provide comprehensive support tailored to each student's needs.

TYPES OF SCHOOLS

Therapeutic services such as speech therapy and counselling are integrated into the school's programme to address students' social, emotional, and developmental needs. Independent schools invest in adaptive resources and facilities like assistive technology and sensory rooms to enhance learning and participation for students with SEN. Despite selective admissions criteria, these schools strive to foster an inclusive environment where all students feel valued and respected. They develop individualised education plans or personalised learning plans for students with SEN, involving parents, teachers, and professionals in regular reviews and updates. Overall, independent schools empower students with SEN to thrive academically, socially, and emotionally by providing tailored support, small class sizes, specialist staff, therapeutic services, adaptive resources, and an inclusive environment.

Alternative provision refers to educational arrangements made for students who, for various reasons, cannot attend mainstream schools full-time. These reasons may include behavioural, medical, psychological, or social challenges that prevent students from accessing education in a traditional school setting. Alternative provision aims to provide these students with educational opportunities and support tailored to their individual needs.

Here are some key points about alternative provision:

Alternative provision encompasses various forms of education outside of mainstream schools, such as alternative schools, pupil referral units (PRUs), home tuition, vocational training, and therapeutic interventions. These initiatives are offered by diverse entities like local authorities, schools, charities, or private organisations. Tailored support is a cornerstone, including personalised learning plans, small group sessions, and access to counselling or therapy. Flexibility characterises the curriculum, accommodating individual needs and interests with academic subjects, vocational training, and life skills development. Transition support aids students moving back to mainstream education or into further education, employment, or training, facilitated by reintegration programmes and mentoring.

Collaboration with mainstream schools, local authorities, and agencies ensures holistic support. Providers monitor and evaluate student progress, tracking academic, attendance, and behavioural indicators to ensure positive outcomes. Overall, alternative provision is crucial in supporting students facing educational challenges, offering tailored support, flexible learning, and collaborative efforts to achieve success.

EOTAS
EDUCATION OTHER THAN AT SCHOOL

During the development of the Children and Families Act 2014 (CFA), Parliament explicitly recognised EOTAS, or education other than school. The education of children and young people for whom attendance at a school or post-16 institution would be unsuitable is specifically covered by law under Section 61 of the 2014 Act. By providing an alternate method of education, EOTAS guarantees that these young people get the appropriate educational opportunities tailored to their needs outside of the conventional school environment.

The child or young person won't need to be registered in or attend a "traditional" educational setting under a formal EOTAS arrangement. Rather, they will receive their education and special education services at home or, in some circumstances, at an outside location that isn't a regular educational establishment.

Elective Home Education (EHE) is not the same as EOTAS. When using an EOTAS package, the provision must be scheduled and paid for by the LA. Should a parent decide to homeschool their child, the LA will not cover any of the expenses or offer any assistance.

Under Section 42 of the Children and Families Act 2014, a local authority is placed under an absolute legal obligation to make sure a child or young person receives all of the provision contained in Section F of their EHCP, unless the circumstances in Section 42(5) are met. Section 42(5) says the obligation is on the LA to provide the EHCP provision unless "the child's parents or the young person has made suitable alternative arrangements."
Special Needs Jungle

Local authorities typically consider EOTAS provision only when they have determined that no other suitable school placements are available. However, it's essential to note that each LA should have its own publicly accessible policy outlining the criteria for eligibility for EOTAS. It is advisable to review the specific policy of the relevant LA to understand the requirements for EOTAS in that area.

MEDIATIONS AND TRIBUNALS
THE PROCESS

SEND mediation is a voluntary process designed to assist parents, schools, and local authorities in resolving disputes related to special educational needs and disabilities in England. It involves an impartial mediator facilitating discussions between the involved parties to reach a mutually agreeable resolution. Mediation can cover various issues such as disagreements over the provision of support, the content of an Education, Health, and Care Plan, or the choice of school placement.

Grounds to mediate include any disagreement between parents and the local authority regarding the special educational provision, health care provision, or social care provision for a child or young person with SEND. This may include disputes related to the local authority's decision not to carry out an EHC needs assessment or issue an EHCP, or disagreements about the content of an EHCP, including the school or other educational institution named in the plan. Mediation can also be requested if there is a disagreement about the type or duration of support specified in the EHCP or if there are concerns about the health or social care provision outlined in the plan.

The process of appealing to the SEND Tribunal allows parents and young people to contest decisions made by local authorities regarding their child's special educational needs and disabilities. Here's an overview:

1. Mediation Request: Before appealing to the SEND Tribunal, parents or young people must attempt mediation to discuss disagreements with the local authority's decision. Mediation aims to resolve issues without a tribunal hearing.

2. Appeal Submission: If mediation doesn't resolve the disagreement, or if it's not pursued, an appeal can be lodged with the SEND Tribunal. This involves completing a tribunal form within a specified timeframe.

3. Case Management: Once lodged, the SEND Tribunal assigns a case manager to review the case, communicate with all parties, and schedule a hearing.

4. Pre-Hearing Preparation: Both parties submit evidence and documents supporting their case, including professional reports and assessments.

5. Tribunal Hearing: The hearing allows both parties to present their case in person to a tribunal panel consisting of a legally qualified chairperson and two specialist members. The panel considers all evidence before reaching a decision.

6. Decision: After deliberation, the tribunal panel communicates their decision in writing, outlining reasons and any further actions required.

7. Appeal Rights: Either party may appeal the tribunal's decision to the Upper Tribunal on a point of law, subject to permission.

In summary, the SEND Tribunal appeal process provides a fair and impartial way to resolve disputes between parents, young people, and local authorities concerning SEND provision.

The Ministry of Justice statistics show that in the academic year 2022/23, HMCTS tribunals recorded 14,000 registered SEN appeals, an increase of 24% when compared to the previous year. Since 2014, the number of appeals has increased every year.

MAKING AN APPEAL

In most cases, you'll need to decide whether to pursue mediation before initiating an appeal. If mediation is chosen or declined, a mediation certificate issued by a mediation provider is required before proceeding with an appeal. You have two months from the date of the final decision letter from the local authority to request this certificate. The mediation provider's deadline cannot be extended. Subsequently, there's an additional 30-day period from the issuance of the mediation certificate to submit an appeal to the SEND Tribunal.

The deadline for lodging appeals is two months from the date of the final written decision letter received from the local authority. Appeals must be submitted to the SEND Tribunal within this timeframe. If there's a need to appeal beyond this deadline due to exceptional circumstances, an application for an extension can be made.

Even after initiating an appeal, it's encouraged for parents, young persons, and the local authority to continue discussions in an attempt to reach agreement on the case.

What grounds are there for appeal?

You have the right to appeal if the local authority:

- Refuses to carry out an Education, Health, and Care EHC Needs assessment for a child or young person's special educational needs, despite a request from the child's parents, the young person, or the educational institution.

- Refuses to issue an EHC Plan for the child or young person following the completion of an EHC Needs assessment.

- Refuses to carry out a reassessment for the child or young person's EHC needs, provided there hasn't been an EHC assessment in the past six months, upon request from the child's parents, the young person, or the educational institution.

- Chooses to cease to maintain an existing EHC plan.

- Refuses to make amendments to the EHC plan following an annual review.

- Refuses not to amend the EHC plan after carrying out a reassessment.

- Finalises or amends a previous EHC plan, and you disagree with any of the following:
  - The section specifying the child or young person's special educational needs (Section B of the EHC Plan).
  - The section outlining special educational provision (Section F of the EHC Plan).
  - The choice of school, college, or institution named in Section I of the EHC Plan, or the type of school specified in Section I.

- The local authority's decision not to name a specific school, college, or institution in Section I of the EHC Plan.

CHANGING ATTITUDES IN SOCIETY

In the United Kingdom, attitudes towards special needs have evolved significantly over time, driven by various factors including legislative changes, social movements, research advancements, and heightened awareness and advocacy efforts. Although there's no pinpointed starting point for these transformations, several critical milestones have shaped how individuals with special needs are perceived:

- Historical Background: Historically, people with disabilities in the UK encountered marginalisation, stigma, and segregation from mainstream society. They were often defined solely by their limitations rather than their capabilities.

- Disability Rights Movements: Similar to global trends, the disability rights movement in the UK played a pivotal role in challenging discrimination and advocating for equal rights and opportunities. This movement shed light on issues of accessibility, inclusivity, and empowerment, influencing societal norms and policies.

- Legislative Reforms: Key legislative changes, such as the introduction of the Disability Discrimination Act (DDA) in 1995 and subsequent updates like the Equality Act 2010, have significantly advanced the rights and protections of individuals with disabilities. These laws promote equal access to services and safeguard against discrimination.

- Inclusive Education: The UK has embraced inclusive education policies, emphasizing the integration of students with disabilities into mainstream schools alongside their non-disabled peers.

- This approach fosters diversity, acceptance, and the belief that all students can thrive with appropriate support.

- Advancements in Understanding: Progress in research, psychology, and neuroscience has deepened our comprehension of disabilities and their impact on individuals. This knowledge has led to more personalised approaches to support, focusing on individual strengths and needs.

- Cultural Shifts: Positive representations of individuals with disabilities in media and popular culture have played a significant role in reshaping societal attitudes. Stories of resilience and empowerment have challenged stereotypes and fostered greater acceptance and understanding.

Despite considerable progress, achieving full inclusion, accessibility, and equality for individuals with disabilities remains an ongoing challenge in the UK. Sustained efforts in advocacy, education, and collaboration are crucial for creating a more inclusive society where everyone has the opportunity to thrive.

In recent times, there's been a noticeable rise in identifying and understanding special needs among young people. This reflects a growing awareness of the wide range of abilities and challenges individuals may have.

AUTISM SPECTRUM DISORDER

Increases in diagnoses have been a feature of Autism for almost as long as it has been a recognised condition: 80 years ago, Autism was thought to affect one in 2,500 children. That has gradually increased and now one in 36 children are believed to have ASD.

What is Autism?

Autism Spectrum Disorder (ASD) is not a disease or illness, it is is a neurodevelopmental disorder that impacts individuals' communication skills, social interactions, and behaviour patterns. People with autism may have difficulties in understanding and interpreting non-verbal cues, expressing emotions, and forming relationships. It is considered a spectrum disorder because its severity and symptoms can vary widely among individuals.

While there is no distinct classification for different "types" of ASD and it can manifest in a variety of ways.

It's important to note that these profiles are not mutually exclusive, and each person on the autism spectrum is unique with their own strengths and challenges.

One of the great and enduring mysteries of Autism is what causes the brain to develop so differently. The behavioural differences of many individuals with Autism are so apparent that it seems intuitive that the causes would also be obvious. Research over the past 70 years has indicated this isn't so.

How is ASD diagnosed?

It is extremely difficult to diagnose ASD, because there are no medical tests that be done. Autism is diagnosed through a combination of behavioural observations, medical history review, developmental screenings, and comprehensive assessments conducted by healthcare professionals specialising in autism evaluation.

As of December 2023, 172,022 people were waiting for an autism assessment in England, according to NHS data. This represents a 47% increase in the number of people waiting within just one year. The National Institute for Health and Care Excellence (NICE) guidance states that no one should wait longer than 13 weeks between being referred and receiving their first assessment1

AUTISM SPECTRUM DISORDER

There are some common traits often associated with Autism.

These may include:

1. Difficulty with social interactions:
Some individuals with autism may struggle with understanding social cues, making eye contact, or building and maintaining relationships.

2. Sensory sensitivities:
Many people with autism may have heightened senses and may be more sensitive to certain sounds, lights, textures, or tastes.

3. Repetitive behaviour's:
Certain repetitive behaviours, such as hand flapping, rocking, or lining up objects, are common among individuals with autism.

4. Special interests:
People with autism may develop intense and specific interests in particular topics, often pursuing them with great enthusiasm and knowledge.

5. Communication challenges:
Some individuals with autism may have difficulty with verbal and non-verbal communication, including challenges with speech, gestures, or understanding figurative language.

6. Routines and predictability:
Many individuals with autism thrive in structured and predictable environments, as they may find comfort and security in routine.

It's important to keep in mind that each person with autism is unique, and these traits can vary greatly in their intensity and presentation.

HOW DOES AUTISM AFFECT LEARNING?

1. Due to the increased sensory sensitivity that Autism frequently causes, the learning environment is very important. Students with Autism can be overwhelmed by bright lights, loud noises, or even particular textures, which makes it difficult for them to participate in class. A classroom that is quieter, accommodating to all senses, has adjustable lighting, and has less distractions can be a more conducive environment for learning.

2. Autism is characterised by social communication problems that affect how people interact with classmates and teachers. It can be difficult to read social signs, keep eye contact, or engage in group activities. Students with autism can feel more at ease in social situations by providing systematic social skills training and encouraging inclusive peer interactions. This will promote healthy relationships and a sense of belonging. Many individuals with ASD exhibit deficits in social skills, such as sharing, taking turns, and empathising with others. These challenges can affect their ability to navigate social situations effectively, resolve conflicts, and establish meaningful connections with peers, contributing to feelings of social exclusion and alienation.

3. Repetitive behaviours and rigid thought processes are common among autistic individuals, and they can interfere with learning. Such behaviours can be challenging in the classroom since they range from resistance to routine adjustments to fixation on particular themes. Students with autism can negotiate their distinctive behaviours and remain interested in learning activities by embracing flexibility in lesson plans, setting clear objectives, and providing support in handling transitions.

According to a 2013 survey by the charity Ambitious About Autism, 60% of teachers in England do not feel that they've received adequate training to teach children with Autism

4. Autism Spectrum Disorders may result in undeveloped executive functioning abilities in people, such as organisation, time management, and impulse control. This may affect their capacity to control their behaviour, manage their workload, and keep on top of assignments. Students with autism can be empowered to become more autonomous learners by developing these skills through the use of visual aids, clear routines, and individualised support.

5. Recent studies have shown that there is limited access to appropriate support services and accommodations when addressing the unique needs of students with Autism in the educational setting. Barriers such as limited availability of specialised resources, inadequate training for educators, and lack of funding can hinder the provision of necessary interventions and accommodations. Without adequate support, students with Autism may struggle to fully participate in educational activities and reach their academic potential.

6. Peer interaction and social dynamics within the classroom can significantly impact learning. Collaborative learning activities, group projects, and peer discussions provide opportunities for knowledge sharing, critical thinking, and social-emotional development. Positive peer relationships can foster a supportive learning community, while social conflicts or bullying may create distractions and emotional distress, inhibiting learning.

PATHOLOGICAL DEMAND AVOIDANCE
PDA

Pathological Demand Avoidance (PDA) is a developmental disorder which is distinct from autism but falls under the spectrum. It is a pervasive developmental disorder (meaning it affects all areas of development) and was first identified by Elizabeth Newson in 2003, although it is still not currently recognised in many tools used for diagnosing autism.

PDA is a complex and often misunderstood condition that many clinicians may overlook or misdiagnose.

It is important to know that PDA is not formally recognised in diagnostic manuals such as the DSM-5 or ICD-10 as a stand-alone diagnosis at this time. Rather, it is frequently referred to as a type of autism spectrum disorder, differentiated by unique behavioural traits associated with avoidance of demands. Ongoing study and discussion within the field relate to the categorisation and understanding of PDA.

PDA may lead a child to exhibit controlling and dominating behaviour, particularly when feeling anxious about losing control. However, when they are in charge of a situation, a child with PDA can present as charming and comfortable.

The PDA Society estimates that 70% of PDA children and young people are not in school, arguing that this is because their needs are not being met.

In comparison to other Autistic individuals, children diagnosed with PDA frequently have better social communication and interpersonal skills. When they are with their classmates, they may also often mimic the actions of authority adults, such teachers.

In school, students with PDA may exhibit avoidance of tasks, manipulative behaviour to avoid demands, social challenges, emotional outbursts, masking behaviour, difficulty with transitions, and sensory sensitivities. Supporting students with PDA in school requires a flexible and individualised approach that focuses on reducing demands, building trust, and providing a supportive environment.

PATHOLOGICAL DEMAND AVOIDANCE
PDA

At home, children with PDA may exhibit extreme avoidance of demands, manipulative behaviour, emotional dysregulation, rigidity, social challenges, and may contribute to parental burnout. Managing PDA at home requires patience, understanding, and collaborative strategies to create a supportive environment.

Understanding the unique aspects of PDA is crucial, as strategies effective for typical Autism may worsen symptoms for those with PDA. Avoidance of ordinary demands due to uncontrolled anxiety, resembling panic attacks, is a primary characteristic. Children may resist tasks even if enjoyable, often responding with "No" and using various tactics to avoid demands.

Children with PDA often display impressive pretend play abilities. They can become deeply engrossed in their imagination, sometimes even mistaking pretend scenarios for reality. This immersion in fantasy can serve as a shield against external demands, which some research has identified as a coping mechanism. Due to these variations from typical autism, children with PDA need tailored support strategies.

How can you help a child with PDA?

1. Using choice and indirect language to lessen the sense of demands is one of two tactics for helping kids with PDA.
2. Using regular routines and visual aids to reduce anxiety and offer predictability.

Is PDA a new condition?

PDA isn't a new condition, but we're hearing more about it now for several reasons:

- Growing Awareness: We're learning more about autism in general, and as we understand it better, we're noticing different types, including PDA, which was first identified by Professor Elizabeth Newson in the 1980s.

- Better Diagnosis: With more research, doctors and specialists can now identify PDA traits more accurately.

- Support Groups: Groups that support parents and carers have been crucial in spreading the word about PDA, offering information and help.

- Recognition: There's a push to include PDA in official autism diagnoses. Many parents and professionals believe it needs to be recognised so children can get the right support.

- Social Media: The internet and social media make it easier to share information. Parents, teachers, and specialists can talk about PDA and spread awareness.

- Educational Focus: Schools are working to be more inclusive, which means they need to understand and support all types of learners, including those with PDA.

ADHD
ATTENTION DEFICIT HYPERACTIVITY DISORDER

What is ADHD?
ADHD is a neurodevelopment disorder and is linked directly to the development of the nervous system.

It causes 'above-normal levels of hyperactive and impulsive behaviours. ADHD is not something that is usually 'grown out of'; this behaviour often continues into adulthood and can affect relationships, friendships and work life.

Children with ADHD may struggle to focus, manage impulsive behaviours (doing without considering the consequences), or exhibit overactive behaviours.

It's important to note that individuals with ADHD may experience symptoms to varying degrees, and not all individuals will display all traits.

Furthermore, symptoms are subject to change over time and can be impacted by a variety of elements, including stress, surroundings, and personal coping mechanisms. A trained healthcare provider should formally diagnose ADHD after doing a thorough assessment of the patient's symptoms and how they affect day-to-day functioning.

Signs and Symptoms

1. **Inattention:** Finding it hard to focus on tasks, getting easily distracted, missing details, and often jumping from one task to another without finishing them.

2. **Hyperactivity:** Feeling restless, constantly moving or fidgeting, like squirming, tapping, or having trouble sitting still when you're supposed to.

3. **Impulsivity:** Acting without thinking, interrupting others, answering questions before they're finished, and struggling to wait your turn.

4. **Disorganisation:** Having trouble keeping things organised, often losing or misplacing items, and finding it tough to follow through with instructions or complete tasks.

5. **Forgetfulness:** Forgetting important things like appointments or deadlines, losing track of time, and failing to finish tasks or chores.

6. **Difficulty with Time Management:** Struggling to manage your time well, underestimating how long tasks will take, putting things off (procrastinating), and frequently being late for appointments or deadlines.

Diagnosing ADHD

ADHD can't be diagnosed with a physical test, like a blood test or an X-ray. Instead, a health professional uses an evaluation process to diagnose it.

ADHD is diagnosed if a child or young person is displaying symptoms of inattentiveness continuously for 6 months, and must be present in multiple settings such as school or. home. These symptoms will also interfere with or reduce daily functioning, and will not be able to be explained by a different condition.

ADHD is divided into 3 different types:
- Inattentive Type: easily distracted, lack of concentration
- Hyperactive/Impulsive Type: blurting out answers, constantly moving
- Combined: showing signs of both

ADHD is often thought of as a childhood condition, but many people reach adulthood without ever being diagnosed. This can happen for several reasons. There is still a lack of awareness about ADHD in adults, and some individuals develop coping mechanisms that hide their symptoms.

ADHD can also be misdiagnosed because its symptoms overlap with other conditions like anxiety and depression. The way ADHD presents itself can vary greatly, and the inattentive type, which is more common in girls and women, is often overlooked.

Cultural stigma and limited access to healthcare can also prevent people from getting a diagnosis.

As a result, many adults only realise they have ADHD when they face new challenges, like starting a new job or university, that make their symptoms more noticeable.

Some people reach adulthood without an ADHD diagnosis for several reasons:

1. **Masking and Coping Mechanisms:** Some individuals develop coping strategies that help them manage or mask their symptoms. These strategies can be effective enough to avoid detection, especially in structured environments like school.
2. **Misdiagnosis:** Symptoms of ADHD can overlap with those of other conditions, such as anxiety, depression, and learning disabilities. As a result, individuals may be misdiagnosed with another condition, leading to the ADHD being overlooked.
3. **Variability in Symptoms:** ADHD symptoms can vary widely and may be less obvious in some people. For instance, those with inattentive ADHD might not display the hyperactive behaviours typically associated with the condition, making it harder to identify.
4. **Gender Differences:** ADHD is often underdiagnosed in girls and women because they are more likely to present with inattentive symptoms rather than hyperactive or impulsive behaviours. This can lead to girls and women being overlooked and not diagnosed until adulthood.
5. **Educational and Societal Factors:** Some individuals may come from environments that do not recognise or support mental health conditions. Cultural stigma, lack of access to healthcare, and socioeconomic factors can all contribute to delayed diagnosis.
6. **Change in Environment:** Some adults may only recognise their symptoms when they encounter new challenges, such as starting university or a new job, where the demands exceed their coping strategies. This can lead to a diagnosis later in life.

DIGGING DEEPER INTO ADHD

Whilst it has only been around since 1987, symptoms of ADHD have been noted by physicians since as early as 1978.

The average age of ADHD diagnosis is 7 years old. ADHD is considered a disability in the UK. ADHD is not on the Autistic Spectrum, but they have some of the same symptoms.

Children with ADHD will often have a difficult time at school if the correct provisions are not put in place.

As well as not being able to stay focused and having poor organisation skills, they may also fail to finish their school work due to the great difficulty in following instructions. They can also be very impatient and always seem to be 'on the go'.

What we should take into account when it comes to ADHD.

- ADHD is a serious neurodevelopment condition that significantly impacts individuals' lives. It is not a matter of mere behaviour or choice but a recognised medical disorder.

- The symptoms of ADHD can appear in children at a young age, causing challenges in their lives. They may seem disinterested or disrespectful, but it's important to understand that they struggle to control their behaviour and attention.

- While attention difficulties are a core aspect of ADHD, the disorder encompasses more than just attention deficits. It involves challenges in impulse control, organisation, time management, and emotional regulation, all of which can profoundly affect daily functioning.

- Individuals with ADHD cannot simply "will" themselves to overcome their symptoms. It is not a matter of choice or lack of effort but rather a neurobiological condition that requires understanding and appropriate support.

- ADHD presents differently in each individual, with symptoms varying widely in severity and manifestation. It is essential to recognise this diversity and avoid generalisations or assumptions about how ADHD affects individuals.

- Support and understanding from others play a crucial role in helping individuals with ADHD navigate their challenges. Empathy, patience, and awareness of the seriousness of ADHD can contribute significantly to fostering a supportive environment for those affected by the disorder.

Michael Phelps is a highly accomplished American swimmer, holding the record for the most Olympic medals won by any athlete. He has openly disclosed his diagnosis of ADHD and has emphasised the importance of managing the condition while pursuing success in his career.

SCHOOL BASED ANXIETY

Stress, concern, or fear that is particularly connected to school-related activities is referred to as "school-based anxiety."
It can cause both physical and mental symptoms, which can have a serious negative effect on wellbeing and academic achievement. Effective treatment of school-related anxiety requires the provision of appropriate support and interventions.

Anxiety is a natural and adaptive response that helps humans cope with stress and potential threats. It is a feeling of unease, apprehension, or worry that can range from mild to severe. Anxiety is a normal part of life and can be a response to various situations, such as facing a challenging task, making an important decision, or encountering a potentially dangerous situation.

School anxiety is a common worry for kids, causing fear or stress about going to school. It can be triggered by various factors like academic pressure, social challenges, or separation anxiety from parents. Symptoms include physical complaints, excessive worry, or avoiding school activities.
This anxiety can affect a child's daily life, leading to difficulty concentrating in class or avoiding social interactions.

Support from parents, teachers, and mental health professionals is crucial. Strategies like creating a supportive environment, gradual exposure to anxiety triggers, teaching relaxation techniques, developing coping skills, and seeking professional help can help kids manage their anxiety and thrive in school.

Physical Symptoms:
- Stomachaches or complaints of physical discomfort.
- Headaches.
- Fatigue and tiredness.
- Muscle tension or restlessness.
- Changes in appetite, either eating more or less than usual.

Emotional Changes:
- Excessive worry or fear about future events.
- Irritability or mood swings.
- Tearfulness or crying.
- Difficulty relaxing or feeling tense.
- Fear of being away from parents or caregivers.

Behavioural Changes:
- Avoidance of certain situations or activities.
- Clinginess, especially in new or unfamiliar environments.
- Difficulty sleeping or frequent nightmares.
- Nail-biting or other nervous habits.

SCHOOL BASED ANXIETY

- Regression in behaviours, such as bedwetting or thumb-sucking.

Cognitive Symptoms:
- Perfectionism and fear of making mistakes.
- Difficulty concentrating or a sense of being easily distracted.
- Overthinking or excessive reassurance-seeking.
- Fearful thoughts about harm coming to oneself or loved ones.

Social Changes:
- Withdrawal from social activities or reluctance to engage with peers.
- Fear of judgment or criticism.
- Difficulty speaking or excessive shyness in social situations.
- Seeking constant approval or reassurance.

School-related Challenges:
- Decline in academic performance.
- Difficulty with focus and attention in class.
- School refusal or reluctance to attend school.

Physical Complaints without Clear Medical Cause:
- Frequent visits to the school nurse with complaints of feeling unwell.
- Resistance to attending school due to physical complaints.

A DAY IN THE LIFE:
SCHOOL BASED ANXIETY

The experience of school-based anxiety varies depending on individual triggers and coping methods. However, it typically involves the following:

1. **Morning Stress:** The day often begins with heightened anxiety as the individual prepares for school, worrying about tests, social interactions, or other school-related challenges.

2. **Physical Symptoms:** Upon arriving at school, physical symptoms like stomachaches, headaches, or a rapid heartbeat may arise, impacting the ability to focus on tasks.

3. **Classroom Challenges:** Throughout the day, concentration difficulties due to racing thoughts or restlessness may make it hard to participate in class discussions or complete assignments, leading to frustration and self-doubt.

4. **Social Pressures:** Interactions with peers can be anxiety-inducing, particularly for those with social skill difficulties or self-consciousness, fearing judgment or rejection and experiencing feelings of isolation.

5. **Coping Strategies:** Despite the challenges, individuals may employ coping strategies such as deep breathing exercises, seeking support from teachers or counsellors, or taking breaks to calm their mind.

6. **End-of-Day Relief:** There may be a sense of relief as the school day ends, but also apprehension about the next day's challenges.

A DAY IN THE LIFE:
SCHOOL BASED ANXIETY

School avoidance

In certain situations, anxiety related to education can result in avoiding school. People who have severe anxiety about going to school may turn to avoidance behaviours as a coping mechanism or to lessen their discomfort. School avoidance may develop over time if the anxiety is not treated or if avoidance behaviours are promoted.

Many children and adolescents experience worries about school, which is normal. However, for some, these concerns can escalate to the point where attending school becomes challenging. If your child is experiencing significant anxiety and struggles to attend school, they may be dealing with Emotionally Based School Avoidance (EBSA).

The COVID-19 pandemic has led to various factors contributing to school avoidance among students. Health concerns, disruption of routines, social isolation, academic challenges, and mental health impacts have all played a role in exacerbating avoidance behaviors. As a result, students may struggle to attend school regularly and require support to overcome these challenges.

EBSA and the law
The Education Act 1996 imposes a legal obligation on parents to ensure their child receives an education and attends school regularly. This law underscores the significance of consistent school attendance for a child's educational progress and well-being.

School avoidance is a significant issue that can impact a child's right to education, with laws varying by region. Parents are typically legally obligated to ensure their child attends school regularly, and chronic avoidance may lead to legal consequences such as fines or intervention from child protective services. Schools are required to provide support and accommodations for students struggling with avoidance due to underlying issues, aiming to address both educational and mental health needs. Collaboration between schools, families, and authorities is essential in addressing school avoidance effectively.

DEVELOPMENTAL CO-ORDINATION DISORDER (DYSPRAXIA)

DCD is a lifelong condition affecting motor skills and coordination, impacting learning despite not being classified as a learning disorder.

Dyspraxia, or Developmental Coordination Disorder (DCD), affects how we move and coordinate tasks. It's like having difficulty tying shoelaces or catching a ball. This condition also impacts balance, making activities like riding a bike challenging. Planning and organisation become tough, too, making multi-step tasks and managing time a struggle.

Dyspraxia can be diagnosed through a comprehensive evaluation by specialists in neurodevelopmental disorders. This includes screenings, medical history reviews, and collaborative assessments by professionals like paediatricians and occupational therapists.

Diagnosis is based on established criteria from standardised classification systems, considering the individual's functional impairment and specific needs.

Estimates suggest that globally, about 5-6% of school-aged children are affected by Dyspraxia, though exact figures vary by region and reporting consistency.

The concept of DCD has been around for quite some time, but its understanding has evolved over the years.

Some parents in the 1970s and 1980s noticed that their child struggled with tasks like tying their shoes, catching a ball, or writing neatly. Back then, it wasn't always clear why some children seemed to have such a tough time with basic movements that others found easy.

As researchers and doctors began to study these challenges more closely, they started to recognise that these difficulties weren't just clumsiness or laziness. They were part of a specific developmental disorder that needed attention and understanding.

In 1994, the official classification as DCD in the DSM marked a significant step forward. It meant that children with Dyspraxia could be properly identified and supported, rather than just being dismissed as slow learners or uncoordinated.

Over time, as awareness has grown, more resources and support have become available for children and adults living with dyspraxia. While there's still progress to be made, the journey from puzzling symptoms to a recognised condition highlights the importance of listening to parents, understanding children's needs, and continually learning about neurodevelopmental disorders.

HOW DOES DCD AFFECT LEARNING?

DCD, can significantly impact learning due to its effects on motor coordination and sensory processing. Here's how dyspraxia can affect learning:

1. Fine and Gross Motor Skills:
Individuals with dyspraxia often struggle with tasks requiring fine motor skills, like writing, typing, or using scissors. Their gross motor skills, such as walking, running, or participating in sports, may also be affected. These challenges can limit involvement in physical education and extracurricular activities, impacting overall physical development.

2. Academic Performance:
Dyspraxia can affect academic tasks involving handwriting, organisation, and spatial awareness. Writing may be slow, messy, and inconsistent, leading to frustration and difficulty expressing ideas. Tasks requiring precise hand-eye coordination, like drawing graphs or diagrams, may also be challenging.

3. Attention and Concentration:
Some individuals with Dyspraxia experience difficulties with attention and concentration, especially in tasks requiring coordination or multiple steps. This affects learning across various subjects as maintaining focus becomes challenging.

4. Sensory Processing:
Many individuals with dyspraxia have sensory processing difficulties, being either hypersensitive or hypersensitive to stimuli like touch, sound, or movement. These sensory issues can disrupt learning environments, making it hard to concentrate in noisy or visually stimulating settings.

5. Social Interaction:
Motor coordination difficulties can impact social interaction and peer relationships. Children with dyspraxia may avoid playground activities or sports, leading to feelings of isolation. Social skills training and supportive environments can help alleviate these challenges.

6. Executive Functioning:
Dyspraxia can affect executive functioning skills such as planning, organising, and time management. Individuals may struggle to sequence tasks or prioritise activities, impacting academic and everyday functioning.

HOW DOES DCD AFFECT LEARNING?

7. Self-esteem and Emotional Well-being: Persistent difficulties with motor coordination and learning tasks can lead to feelings of frustration, low self-esteem, and anxiety. It's crucial for educators and caregivers to provide positive reinforcement, accommodations, and support to enhance self-confidence and emotional resilience.

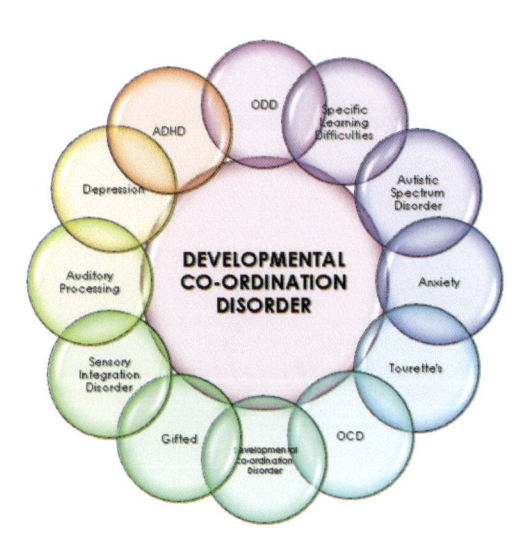

DCD and Dyspraxia both describe difficulties with motor skills and coordination, but dyspraxia specifically focuses on problems with motor planning and execution, while DCD is a broader term covering various coordination difficulties without pinpointing the cause. Essentially, they refer to similar challenges with movement but may differ in their diagnostic criteria and emphasis on specific aspects of motor function.

DYSCALCULIA

Dyscalculia is a math learning disability where individuals struggle with various mathematical concepts and operations. This difficulty can range from understanding basic concepts like size comparison to solving both simple and complex math problems.
It can often occur with other conditions such as dyslexia or ADHD.

Dyscalculia is frequently misunderstood. It's possible that a lot of people in the UK are unaware of the phrase or the difficulties it poses. Dyscalculia is sometimes misdiagnosed as being merely "bad at maths" or as the result of inattention or disinterest. It's a particular kind of learning disability with neurological origins that impairs a person's capacity to understand and use numbers. People who have dyscalculia have difficulty receiving the help and accommodations they require to excel in school and in daily life as a result of this misconception. It is essential to increase awareness regarding dyscalculia and offer suitable tools and solutions to individuals impacted by the condition.

Experts estimate that Dyscalculia affects between 3% and 7% of people worldwide.

Supporting someone with dyscalculia involves understanding their challenges, providing personalised instruction, breaking down concepts, using alternative teaching methods, offering positive reinforcement, advocating for accommodations, creating a supportive environment, collaborating with professionals, building confidence, and raising awareness about dyscalculia. These strategies aim to address the unique needs of individuals with dyscalculia and empower them to succeed academically and personally.

Emotional symptoms of Dyscalculia

1. Dyscalculia can lead to frustration due to difficulty understanding mathematical concepts and performing calculations.

2. Individuals with dyscalculia may experience anxiety related to math tasks and assessments, leading to avoidance behaviours.

3. Persistent math difficulties can lower self-confidence and self-worth, contributing to feelings of inadequacy.

4. Dyscalculia may cause feelings of shame or embarrassment about math difficulties, particularly in academic or social settings.

5. Some individuals with dyscalculia may avoid math-related tasks or situations to cope with anxiety and discomfort.

6. Pressure to perform in math-related situations can increase stress levels for individuals with dyscalculia.

7. Dyscalculia may lead to social withdrawal and feelings of isolation as individuals struggle to relate to peers.

8. Prolonged struggles with math can contribute to feelings of hopelessness and depression in individuals with dyscalculia.

DYSLEXIA

What is it?

Dyslexia is a type of learning difficulty that impacts how people read and understand language. It can cause difficulties in accurately reading, spelling, and comprehending written text, even if someone has normal intelligence and access to good education.

Working with language is difficult for many people who have dyslexia. According to some experts, five to ten percent of persons are affected. There are others who claim that up to 17% of people exhibit symptoms of reading difficulties.
People with Dyslexia are affected differently. Therefore, symptoms may differ from person to person.

Dyslexia is quite common among students, affecting about 5-10% of people worldwide. That means in a typical classroom, there's a good chance that at least one student might have dyslexia.

It doesn't matter where you're from or what your background is - Dyslexia can affect anyone. Early identification and getting the right help are really important for students with dyslexia. With the right support, they can do just as well as their peers.

How does it affect learning:

1. **Reading:** Dyslexia makes it hard to read accurately and fluently. People with dyslexia may struggle to recognise and understand written words, which slows down their reading speed and comprehension. They might find it tough to sound out words phonetically or identify common sight words.

2. **Writing and Spelling:** Dyslexia often affects spelling and writing skills. Individuals may have trouble spelling words correctly, remembering the right order of letters, or organising their thoughts on paper. Dysgraphia, which often goes hand in hand with dyslexia, involves difficulties with handwriting and expressing thoughts in writing.

3. **Language Processing:** Dyslexia can impact language processing, making it challenging to understand spoken language, follow instructions, or express thoughts verbally. Some individuals struggle with auditory processing, finding it hard to differentiate similar-sounding words or follow oral directions.

4. **Working Memory:** Dyslexia can affect working memory, which is crucial for holding and manipulating information. This makes it difficult to follow multi-step instructions, remember information while reading or writing, or recall information later on.

SPEECH & LANGUAGE DISORDERS

Speech and language disorders cover a range of challenges that affect how people communicate. These issues can include trouble with speaking clearly, understanding language, or socialising. Speech disorders might cause someone to stutter or have difficulty pronouncing certain sounds, while language disorders could make it hard to express thoughts or understand what others are saying. Getting help early and working with a therapist can make a big difference in improving communication skills and making life easier for those affected.

Speech and language disorders are diagnosed by qualified professionals like speech-language pathologists. These experts conduct thorough assessments involving interviews, tests, and observations to determine if an individual has a disorder. Early diagnosis and intervention are vital for effective management. If someone suspects they or someone they know has a speech and language disorder, seeking evaluation from a licensed healthcare provider is important.

Two interventions for students with Speech and Language Disorders are:

1. **Speech and Language Therapy:** This intervention involves working with a qualified speech and language therapist who provides tailored therapy sessions to address specific speech and language goals. These sessions may include activities targeting speech production, language comprehension, vocabulary development, and social communication skills.

2. **Augmentative and Alternative Communication (AAC):** For students with severe speech impairments, AAC interventions involve using tools and devices such as communication boards, picture exchange systems, or speech-generating devices to support and enhance communication. These interventions aim to empower students to express themselves effectively and participate more fully in academic and social activities.

SPEECH & LANGUAGE DISORDERS

One tip to support someone with a Speech and Language disorder is to practice active listening, offering them extra time to communicate without pressure. Using visual aids and non-verbal cues can also aid understanding. Patience, empathy, and encouragement are essential for creating a supportive environment that helps individuals with speech and language disorders communicate confidently.

Involving parents and caregivers in therapy sessions and providing strategies for home practice can reinforce skills learned in therapy and support generalisation of skills to everyday settings.

It's important for interventions to be evidence-based, individualised, and implemented by qualified professionals. Additionally, early intervention is key for maximising outcomes and supporting the overall development and well-being of individuals with speech and language disorders.

FACT

Samuel L. Jackson had a stuttering problem when he was young. Despite this challenge, he overcame it through hard work and perseverance, eventually becoming one of Hollywood's most iconic and recognisable voices!

SENSORY PROCESSING DISORDER (SPD)

The term "sensory processing disorder" describes the incapacity to effectively employ information received from the senses in order to go about daily activities. SPD is an all-encompassing phrase that encompasses a range of neurological problems rather than any one particular illness.

SPD can affect people in many ways. They may have extreme reactions to sensory input such as touch, sound, taste, smell, or sight. SPD can manifest in various ways, impacting students' ability to regulate their responses and participate in academic, social, and daily life activities. It can affect their attention, behavior, and overall functioning in the classroom and beyond.

Signs and Symptoms:
In our classrooms, we may observe students showing signs of hypersensitivity or hyposensitivity to sensory stimuli, such as touch, sound, sight, taste, or smell. They might struggle with regulating their responses to sensory input, leading to behaviors like seeking or avoiding certain sensations. These challenges can significantly impact their ability to focus, engage, and participate in learning activities.

Impact on Learning and Behaviour:
Students with SPD often face obstacles in their learning journey. Sensory sensitivities can make it difficult for them to concentrate, resulting in distractibility or avoidance of certain tasks. Additionally, these students may experience heightened stress or anxiety in sensory-rich environments, affecting their academic performance and social interactions. It's also important to recognise how sensory processing difficulties can influence their motor skills and self-regulation.

Support and Intervention:
As teachers, we play a crucial role in supporting students with SPD. By creating a classroom environment that accommodates their sensory needs, we can help them thrive. This might involve reducing sensory distractions, providing accommodations like sensory breaks, or collaborating with specialists such as occupational therapists to develop personalised intervention plans.

Promoting Awareness and Understanding:
Increasing awareness of SPD among family and friends, colleagues, students, and school community is essential. By educating ourselves and others about the signs and impact of SPD, we can create a more inclusive and supportive environment for our students. Recognising their unique challenges and providing them with the support they need is key to fostering their academic success and overall well-being.

Understanding sensory processing disorders allows us to better support our students and create an inclusive learning environment where all students can succeed. By implementing targeted interventions, promoting awareness, and fostering understanding, we can make a positive difference in the lives of students with SPD, helping them reach their full potential in our classrooms and beyond.

In the UK, SPD is typically diagnosed through a comprehensive assessment conducted by qualified healthcare professionals, such as occupational therapists, paediatricians, or child psychologists. The assessment process may involve gathering information from parents, caregivers, and teachers about the individual's sensory experiences and behaviours in different settings.
Standardised assessments and observations are often used to evaluate sensory processing abilities and identify any challenges or difficulties.

VISUAL IMPAIRMENT

What is a Visual Impairment?

A visual impairment refers to a condition where a person's vision is significantly compromised, making it difficult for them to see or interpret visual information. This impairment can range from mild to severe and may result from various factors such as eye diseases, injuries, or congenital conditions. Visual impairments can affect different aspects of vision including acuity (sharpness), field of vision, color perception, and depth perception. It can impact a person's ability to perform daily activities, navigate their environment, and participate in educational or professional settings. People with visual impairments often use assistive devices or adaptive strategies to enhance their independence and access to information.

Some diagnosed visual impairments include:

- Myopia: Difficulty seeing distant objects clearly.
- Hyperopia: Difficulty seeing close objects clearly.
- Astigmatism: Blurred or distorted vision caused by an irregularly shaped cornea.
- Amblyopia: Reduced vision in one eye due to abnormal development in childhood.
- Strabismus: Misalignment of the eyes, affecting depth perception and coordination.
- Cataracts: Clouding of the eye's lens, leading to blurred or dim vision.
- Glaucoma: Increased pressure within the eye, damaging the optic nerve and causing vision loss.

A student with a visual impairment can be supported in several ways

- **Access to Appropriate Resources:** Ensure the student has access to necessary resources such as braille materials, large print books, audio recordings, or assistive technology devices like screen readers or magnifiers.

- **Specialised Instruction:** Provide specialised instruction in areas such as orientation and mobility training, independent living skills, and assistive technology training to enhance the student's independence and academic success.

- **Environmental Adaptations:** Make environmental adaptations in the classroom, such as providing preferential seating, ensuring good lighting, minimising visual clutter, and using tactile markers or auditory cues to aid navigation and orientation.

- **Peer Support and Inclusion:** Foster a supportive and inclusive classroom environment where peers are educated about visual impairments and encouraged to provide support and inclusion to the student with a visual impairment.

- **Regular Monitoring and Review:** Regularly monitor the student's progress, assess the effectiveness of support strategies, and review their individualised learning plan to ensure it remains relevant and responsive to their evolving needs.

- **Emotional and Social Support:** Provide emotional and social support to address any challenges or concerns the student may face related to their visual impairment, including opportunities for peer interaction and support from school counsellors or specialists.

- **Parental Involvement:** Involve parents or caregivers in the development and implementation of support strategies, ensuring open communication, collaboration, and shared decision-making to support the student's overall well-being and academic success.

ATTACHMENT DISORDER

'Attachment issues can arise for a number of reasons, but they are typically rooted in childhood experiences.'

An attachment disorder stemming from early life experiences and disruptions in the caregiver-child bond can severely hinder a child's ability to engage in learning. Children affected by attachment disorder often struggle with trust, emotional regulation, and forming secure relationships, all of which can impede their learning progress.

These challenges may manifest in the classroom as difficulties in forming connections with teachers and peers, managing emotions in response to social or academic stressors, and adhering to classroom rules and routines. Consequently, children with attachment disorder may exhibit behavioural issues and disruptions in their learning, potentially leading to the identification of special educational needs.

Attachment disorder is a spectrum. Some children are more seriously impacted than others, as is the case with many disorders.

Learning can be severely impacted by attachment issues in a number of ways.

Emotional Control: Children with attachment disorders may find it difficult to control their feelings, which makes it tough for them to handle stress, worry, and annoyance. These emotional difficulties may make it difficult for them to concentrate and pay attention in class.

Social Skills: Children with attachment issues may have difficulty forming healthy relationships with their classmates and developing social skills. They might have trouble with social skills like cooperating, sharing, and taking turns—all of which are necessary for effective learning in group environments.

Trust Issues: Children with attachment disorders frequently struggle to build trustworthy relationships with adults, teachers included. It may be difficult for educators to involve them in learning activities because of this lack of trust, which can lead to resistance to advice and instruction.

Behaviour Issues: Children with attachment issues may display aggressive, defiant, or withdrawing behaviours in the classroom. These actions may cause disturbances and diversions, which may have a detrimental effect on both their own and their peers' learning.

Academic Performance: Children may struggle academically as a result of the emotional, social, and behavioural issues related to attachment disorders. Due to erratic attendance or participation, they could fail to finish assignments, have reduced academic self-esteem, and have learning gaps.

ACRONYMS

Navigating the world of special needs education can feel like learning a whole new language because of all the acronyms used. These acronyms help simplify conversations between professionals, parents, and teachers, but they can be overwhelming if you're not familiar with them. Knowing these abbreviations is key to effectively supporting and advocating for kids with special needs. By getting to know the most common acronyms, you can better understand the education system, find the right resources, and make sure kids get the support they need.

Here is a list of the most used acronyms in SEN:

1. SEN - Special Educational Needs
2. SEND - Special Educational Needs and Disabilities
3. IEP - Individualised Education Plan
4. EHCP - Education, Health, and Care Plan
5. ASD - Autism Spectrum Disorder
6. ADHD - Attention Deficit Hyperactivity Disorder
7. LD - Learning Disability
8. SLD - Severe Learning Difficulties
9. MLD - Moderate Learning Difficulties
10. PDD - Pervasive Developmental Disorder
11. OT - Occupational Therapy
12. SALT - Speech and Language Therapy
13. BESD - Behavioural, Emotional and Social Difficulties
14. EP - Educational Psychologist
15. ABA - Applied Behaviour Analysis
16. AAC - Augmentative and Alternative Communication
17. DSP - Designated Special Provision
18. CAMHS - Child and Adolescent Mental Health Services
19. SEMH - Social, Emotional, and Mental Health
20. PDA - Pathological Demand Avoidance

BIBLIOGRAPHY AND REFERENCES

https://www.masters-in-special-education.com/lists/5-most-common-learning-disabilities/

https://anorexiafamily.com/meals-anxiety-school-eating-disorder/?v=79cba1185463

https://explore-education-statistics.service.gov.uk/find-statistics/special-educational-needs-in-england

https://images.pearsonclinical.com/images/assets/basc-3/basc3resources/DSM5_DiagnosticCriteria_ADHD.pdf

https://targetjobs.co.uk/careers-advice/job-descriptions/279191-teacher-special-educational-needs-job-description

https://sunshine-support.org/eotas-5-things-you-need-to-know/

https://www.aep.org.uk/training/want-to-be-an-ep/

https://sunshine-support.org/eotas-5-things-you-need-to-know/

https://www.supportincornwall.org.uk/kb5/cornwall/directory/advice.page?id=O2_yvvh136Y

https://www.nhs.uk/mental-health/conditions/anorexia/treatment/

https://www.beateatingdisorders.org.uk/types/anorexia

https://www.verywellmind.com/what-is-an-attachment-disorder-4580038

https://www.highspeedtraining.co.uk/hub/how-to-support-a-child-with-autism-in-the-classroom/

https://childlawadvice.org.uk/information-pages/special-educational-needs

https://www.webmd.com/brain/autism/how-do-doctors-diagnose-autism

https://www.gov.uk/children-with-special-educational-needs/extra-SEN-help

https://www.england.nhs.uk/learning-disabilities/care/children-young-people/send

https://www.goodschoolsguide.co.uk/special-educational-needs/your-rights/sen-but-no-ehcp

https://schoolleaders.thekeysupport.com/pupils-and-parents/sen/managing/the-sen-code-of-practice-a-summary/

https://www.hopkinsmedicine.org/health/conditions-and-diseases/adhdadd

https://engage-education.com/blog/the-send-code-of-practice/

https://www.specialneedsjungle.com/eotas-education-otherwise-than-at-school-what-is-it-and-can-i-get-it/

https://www.parentingspecialneeds.org/article/17-popular-quotes

https://sunshine-support.org/ehcps-myths/#:~:text="A%20child%20needs%20to%20be,targeting%20a%20child's%20intellectual%20ability.

https://www.nidirect.gov.uk/articles/special-educational-needs-step-by-step-approach

https://www.healthcareers.nhs.uk/explore-roles/allied-health-professionals/roles-allied-health-professions/speech-and-language-therapist

https://www.worcester.ac.uk/courses/national-award-senco-nasenco-pg-cert-education-special-educational-needs-coordination#course-content

https://lifewithasideoftheunexpected.com/special-needs-quotes/

https://nationalcareers.service.gov.uk/job-profiles/special-educational-needs-(sen)-teaching-assistant

https://www.theschoolrun.com/how-a-senco-could-help-your-child

https://www.goodschoolsguide.co.uk/special-educational-needs/schools-and-sen/senco

https://www.prospects.ac.uk/job-profiles/educational-psychologist

https://www.verywellmind.com/diagnosis-of-adhd-20584

https://sendadvicesurrey.org.uk/what-is-the-send-code-of-practice/

https://www.healthline.com/health/adhd/three-types-adhd

THANK YOU!

In the world of SEND, there are countless incredible individuals, organisations, and businesses making a difference every day.

I would like to take this opportunity to thank all the support groups and organisations who work tirelessly to support local authorities and families. Their steadfast commitment to supporting families, raising awareness at the highest levels, and advocating for children and young people with SEND is incredibly motivating.

Above all, I want to express my deepest appreciation for our children and young people who have a wide range of needs. They deserve understanding, support, and care throughout their entire lives—not just during their years in education.

As we continue on this journey, let's remember that each small step forward brings us closer to a brighter future for SEND.

Together, we can make a meaningful difference in the lives of those with the most unique needs.

Thank you for reading this book.

Candace xx

Together We Can!

Printed in Great Britain
by Amazon